36

32

42 44

48

54 Mumbai

56 Bangkok

58 Hong Kong

60 Seoul

62 Tokyo

64 Jakarta

50

52

66 Sydney

68 Auckland

58

56

54

60

62

64

66

68

KEY

 Population (city and surrounding area)

Language

Country

For Catherine

BIG PICTURE PRESS

First published in the UK in 2016 by Big Picture Press,
part of the Bonnier Publishing Group,
The Plaza, 535 King's Road, London, SW10 0SZ
www.bigpicturepress.net
www.bonnierpublishing.com

First edition 2015
© Benoit Tardif
Published with the permission of Comme des géants inc.,
6504, av. Christophe-Colomb
Montreal (Quebec) H2S 2G8
All rights reserved.
Translation rights arranged through VeroK Agency, Spain

Design copyright © 2015 by Comme des géants inc
English translation copyright © 2016 by The Templar Company Limited

10 9 8 7 6 5 4 3 2 1
0316 008

ISBN 978-1-78370-571-9

Written by Lise Duquette
Content collaborated by Nadine Robert
English language edition edited by Isobel Boston

Printed in China

Populations are approximate.

Benoit Tardif

METROPOLIS

BPP

MONTREAL

👤 4 million 💬 French / English 🚩 Canada

Notre-Dame Basilica

bagel stand

Clock Tower (45m)

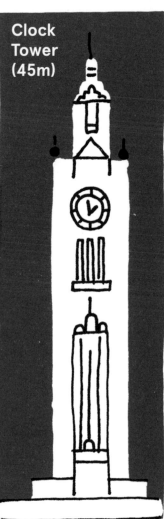

ice hockey player

theme park

6

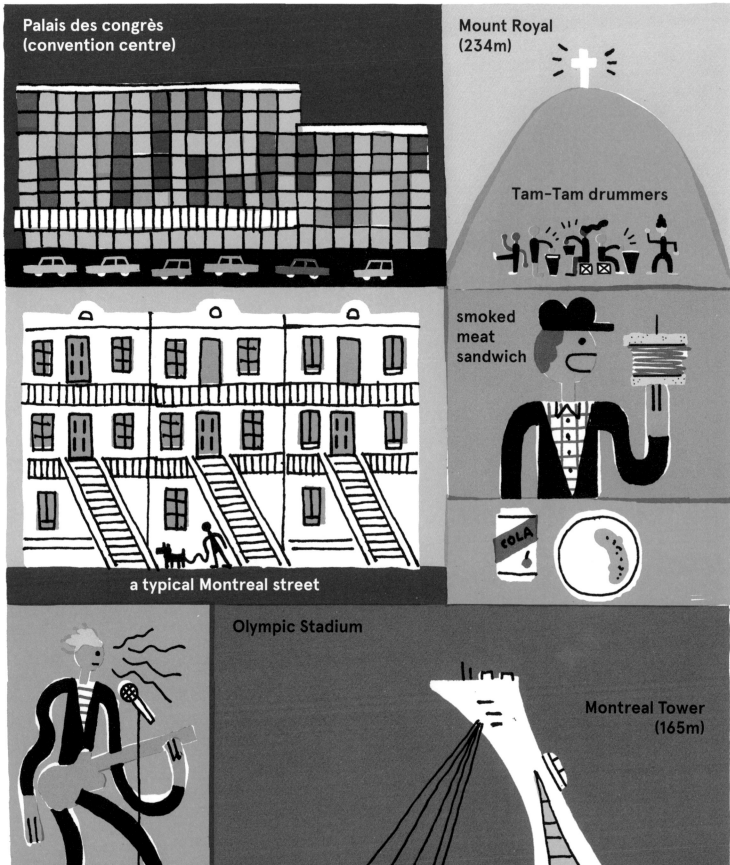

Palais des congrès
(convention centre)

Mount Royal
(234m)

Tam-Tam drummers

smoked
meat
sandwich

COLA

a typical Montreal street

Olympic Stadium

Montreal Tower
(165m)

rock singer

7

TORONTO

👤 6 million　💬 English / French　🏳 Canada

blue jay
blue jay

CN Tower (553m)

Stanley Cup in the Hockey Hall of Fame

Royal Canadian Mounted Police

walk on the waterfront

Rogers Centre (sports stadium)

Lake Ontario

City Hall

GO!GO!GO!

ice hockey player

ice rink

doughnut stand

Royal Ontario Museum
(natural history)

NEW YORK

 23.6 million   English   United States of America

Empire State Building (381m)

Chrysler Building (319m)

baseball player

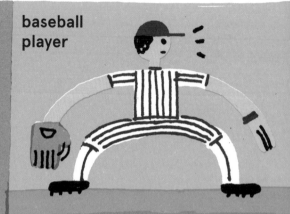

hot dog stand

Guggenheim Museum

traffic on 42nd Street

CHICAGO

👤 10 million 　💬 English 　🚩 United States of America

Marina City Towers (179m)

Buckingham Fountain

blues musician

The Wrigley Building

cruise on the Chicago river

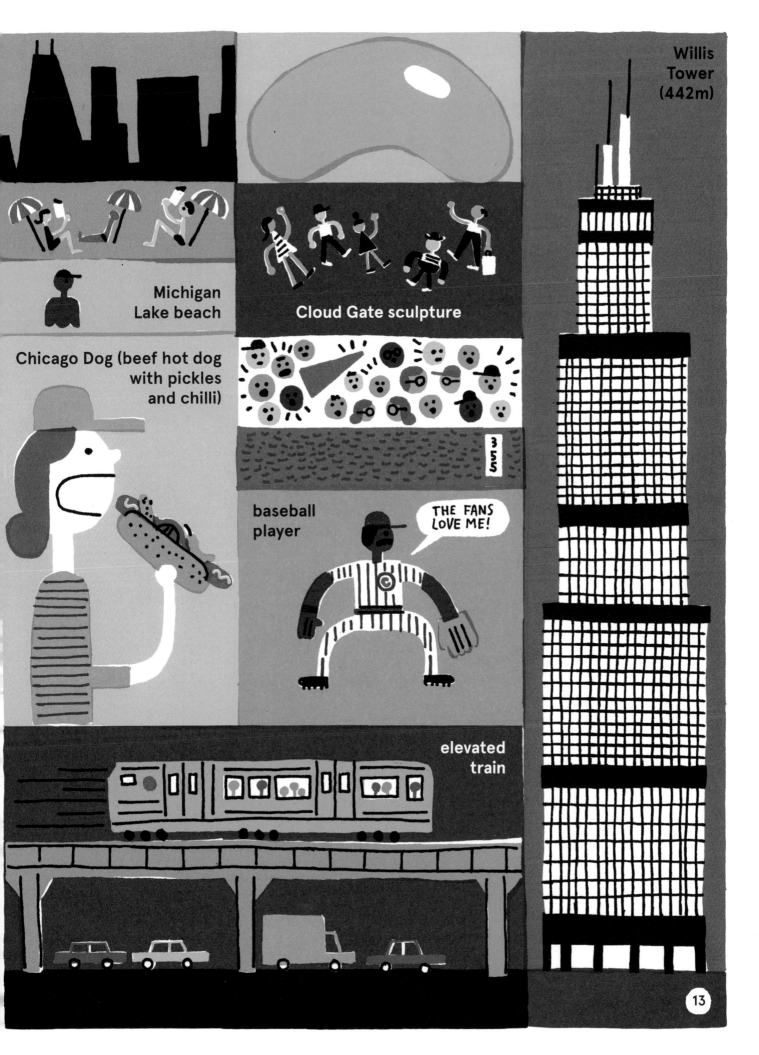

SAN FRANCISCO

 8.6 million   💬 English   🚩 United States of America

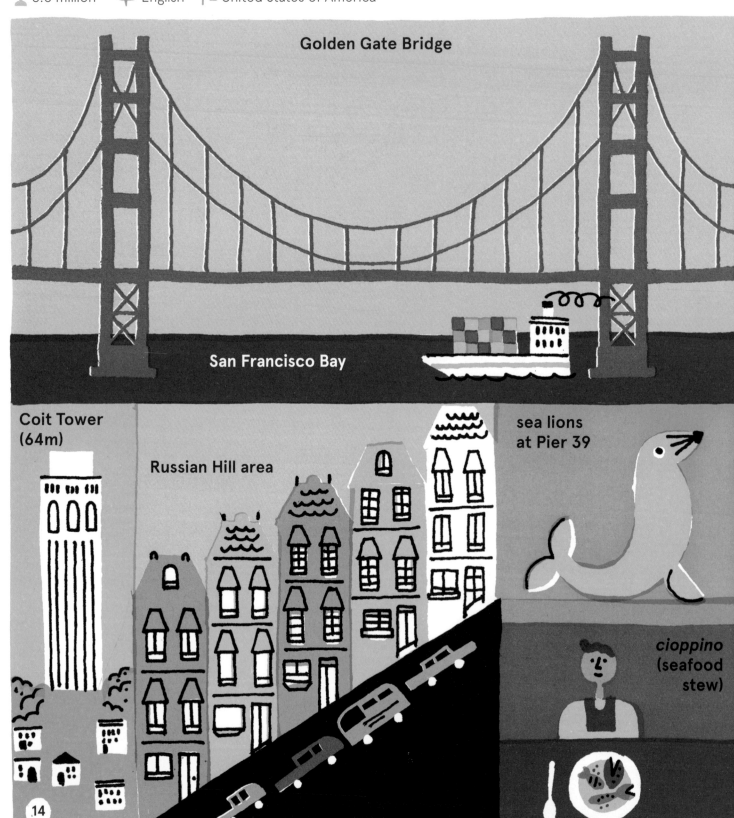

Golden Gate Bridge

San Francisco Bay

Coit Tower (64m)

Russian Hill area

sea lions at Pier 39

cioppino (seafood stew)

14

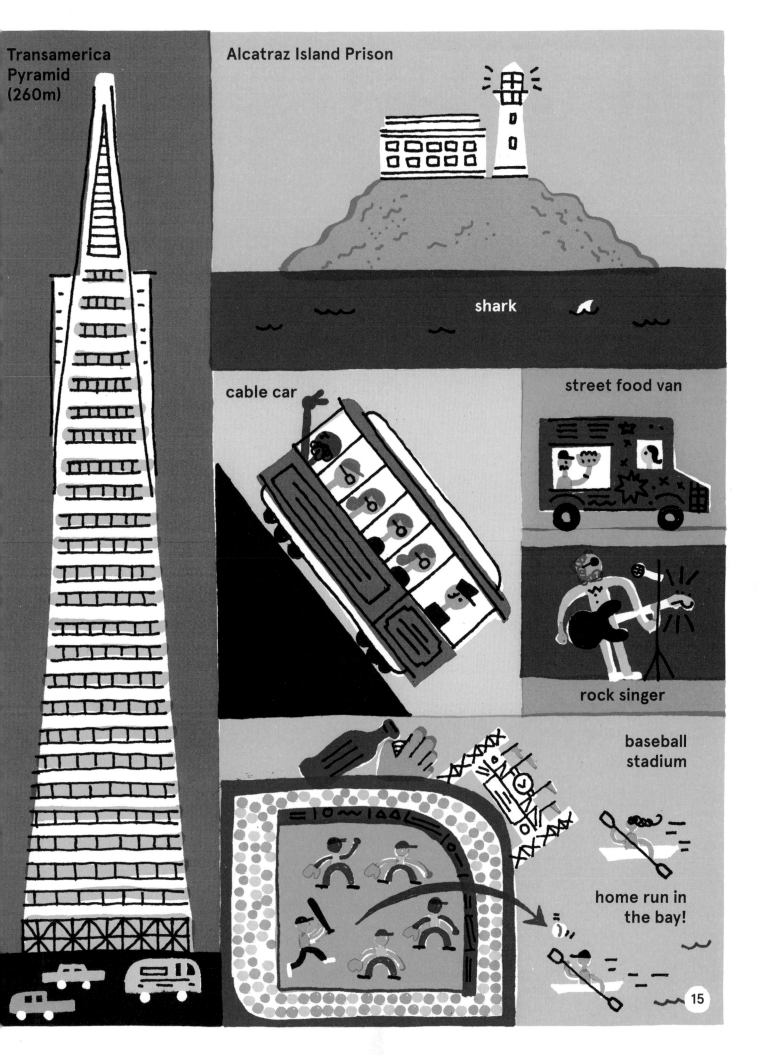

Transamerica
Pyramid
(260m)

Alcatraz Island Prison

shark

cable car

street food van

rock singer

baseball
stadium

home run in
the bay!

MEXICO
CITY

👤 20 million 💬 Spanish 🏳 Mexico

Mexico City Metropolitan Cathedral

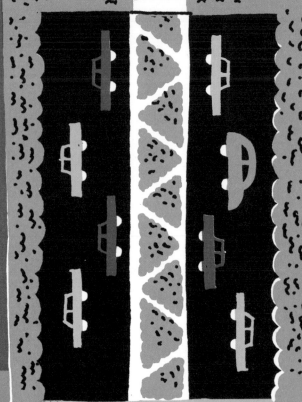

Paseo de la Reforma (main avenue)

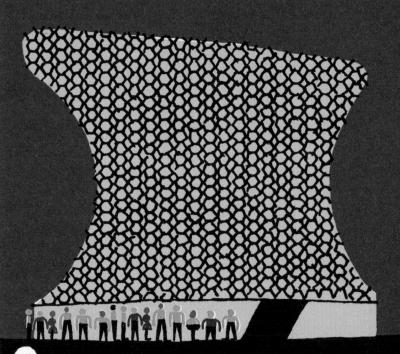

Soumaya Museum

pambazos (sandwich filled with chorizo and potato)

green taxi

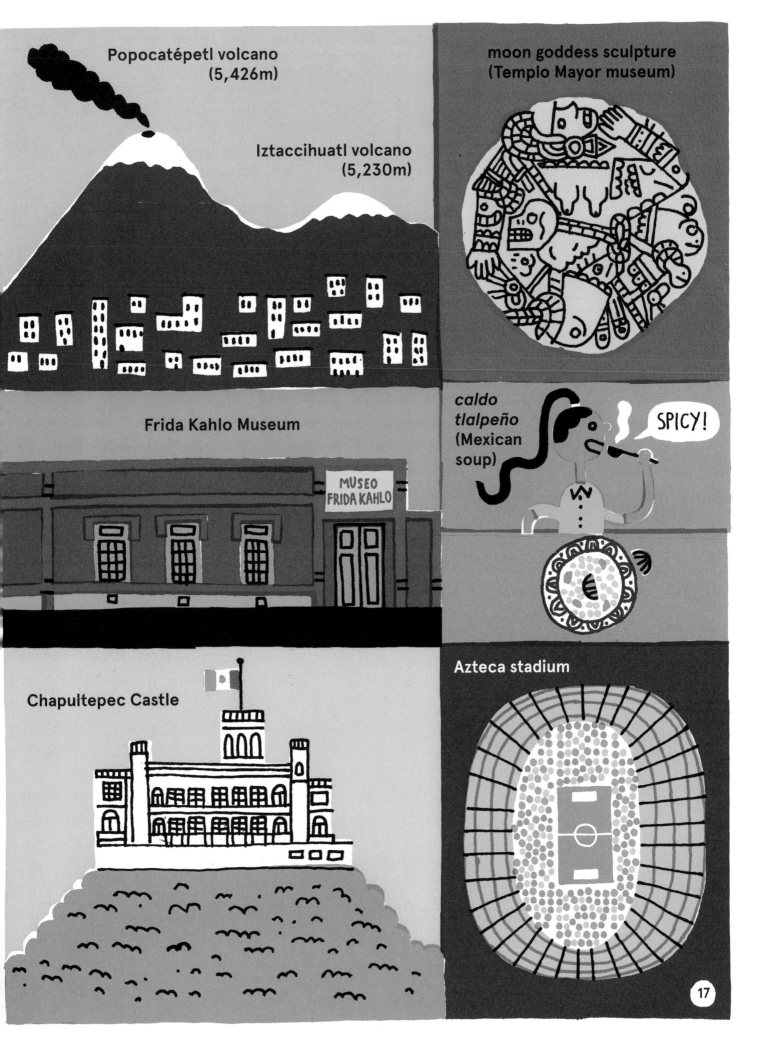

RIO DE JANEIRO

👤 12 million 💬 Portuguese 🏴 Brazil

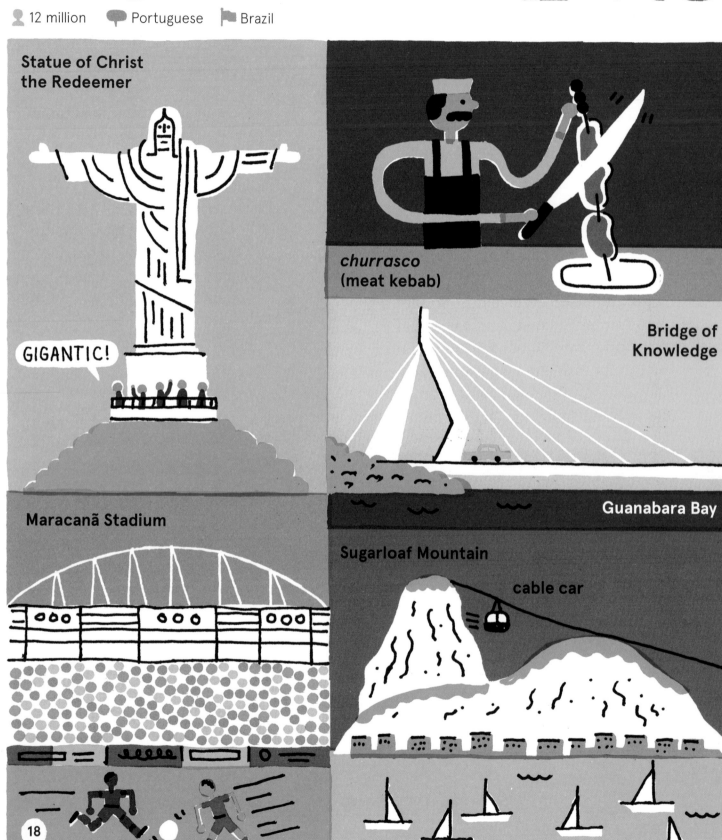

Statue of Christ the Redeemer

GIGANTIC!

churrasco (meat kebab)

Bridge of Knowledge

Guanabara Bay

Maracanã Stadium

Sugarloaf Mountain

cable car

BUENOS AIRES

👤 14 million   💬 Spanish   🚩 Argentina

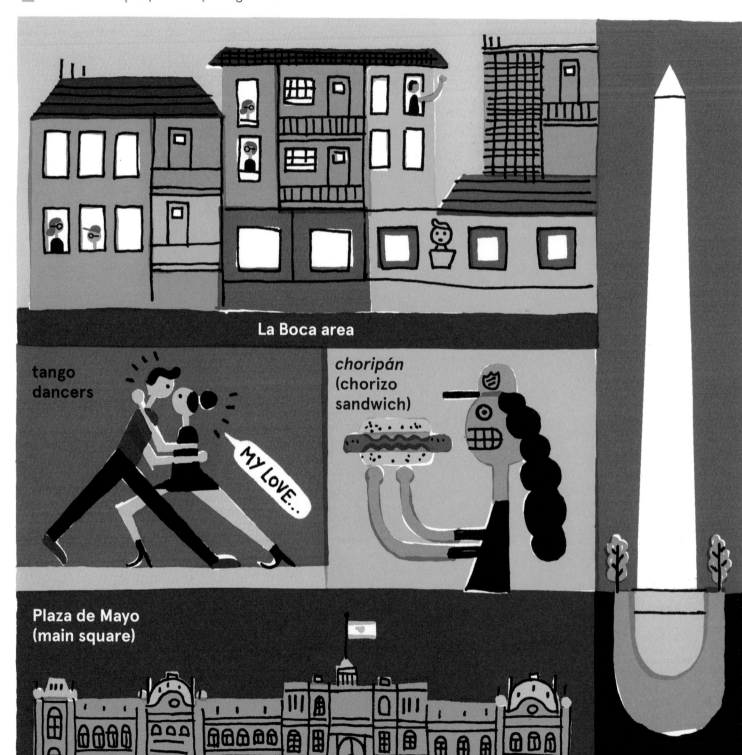

La Boca area

tango dancers

choripán (chorizo sandwich)

MY LOVE...

Plaza de Mayo (main square)

Obelisk of Buenos Aires (68m)

20

monuments at La Recoleta Cemetery

Colón Theatre

Floralis Genérica Sculpture

football player

Buenos Aires Zoo

Puente de la Mujer (rotating footbridge)

Puerto Madero waterfront

LONDON

👤 13.7 million   💬 English   🏳 United Kingdom

telephone box

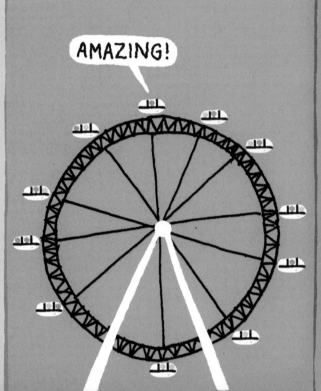

London Eye

30 St Mary Axe skyscraper
(180m)

  tube sign

double-decker bus

'The Gherkin'

PARIS

 12.3 million   French   France

newspaper kiosk

gendarme (police officer)

French baguette

Eiffel Tower (324m)

Arc De Triomphe

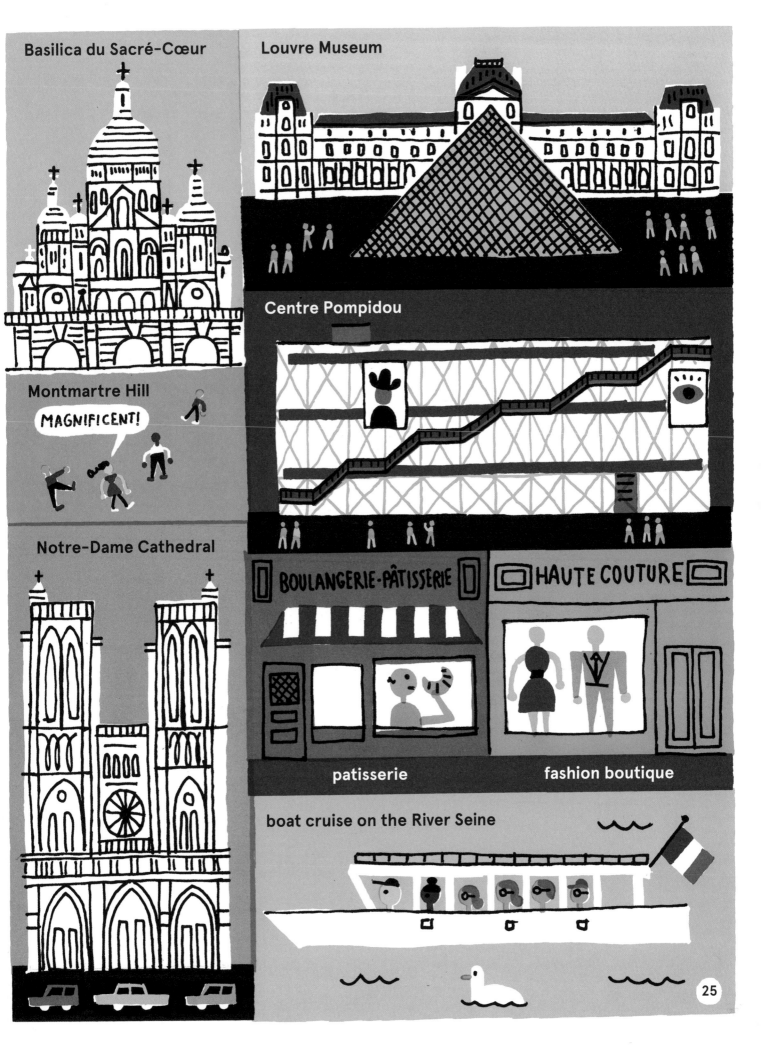

AMSTERDAM

tulip

👤 2.3 million 💬 Dutch 🏴 Netherlands

Amsterdam Centraal Station

windmill brewery

cyclists along the canals

canal

stroopwafel
(syrup waffle)

26

row of townhouses

Rembrandt, Van Gogh and Vermeer
paintings at the Rijksmuseum

bike taxi

TO VONDELPARK, PLEASE!

football
player

patat
oorlog

(fries,
mayonnaise,
peanut sauce
and onions)

flower market

27

ZURICH

 1.3 million   German   Switzerland

Grossmünster church

Zurich Opera House

Uetliberg Mountain (871m)

Uto Kulm Hotel

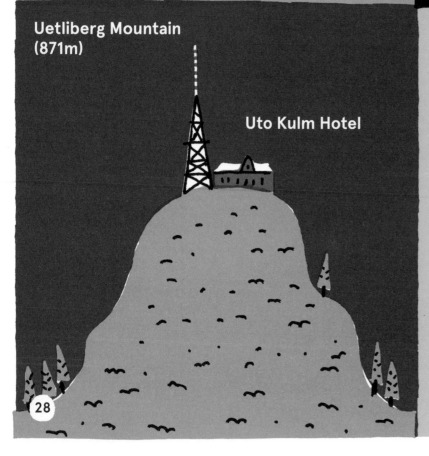

swimming in the Limmat river

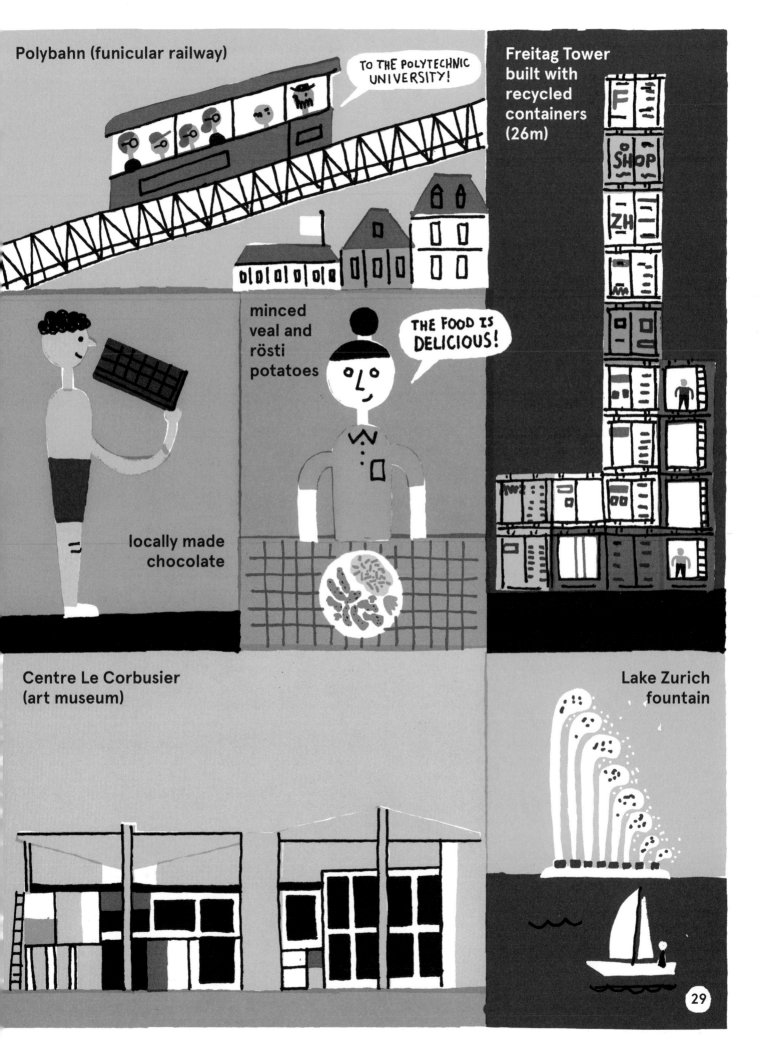

BERLIN

 4.4 million 💬 German 🏳 Germany

döner kebab

TV Tower

Reichstag Palace
(German parliament building)

painted bear sculptures

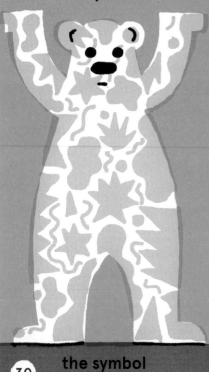

(30) **the symbol of Berlin**

Brandenburg Gate

Fernsehturm (368m)

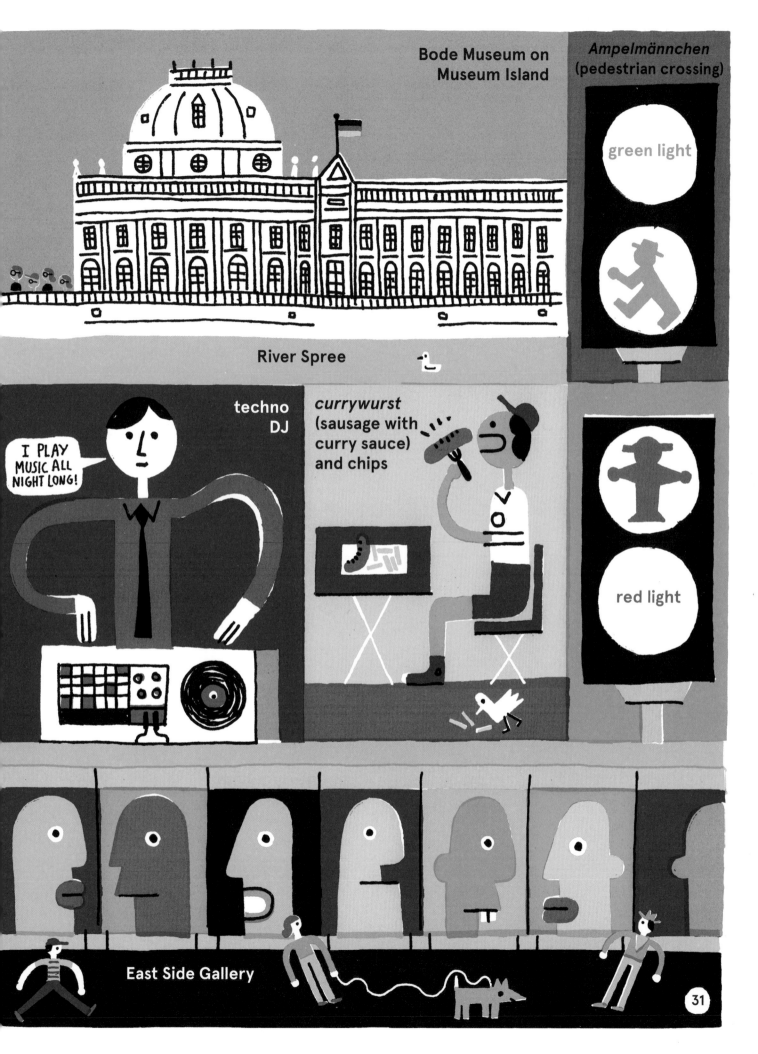

KRAKÓW

 1.5 million Polish Poland

Kraków Cloth Hall

Saint Mary's Basilica

bell ringer

St. Florian's Gate

sightseeing by golf cart

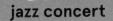

jazz concert

obwarzanek **(bread plait)**

Wawel Royal Castle

Wawel Dragon statue

salt sculpture at Wieliczka Salt Mine

pierogis
(pasta stuffed with meat or vegetables)

Father Bernatek Footbridge

Vistula River

STOCKHOLM

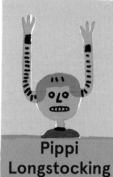

Pippi Longstocking

 2.2 million   Swedish   Sweden

Royal Palace

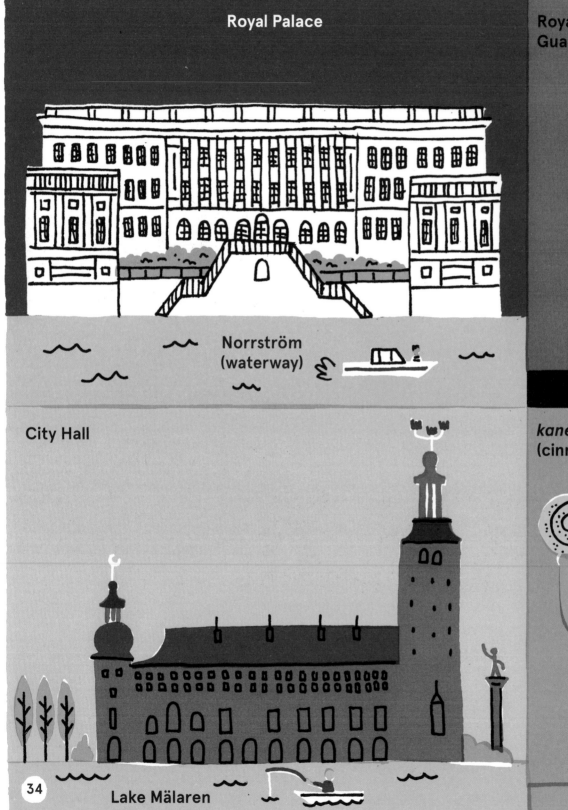

Norrström
(waterway)

Royal Palace Guard

kanelbulle
(cinnamon roll)

City Hall

Lake Mälaren

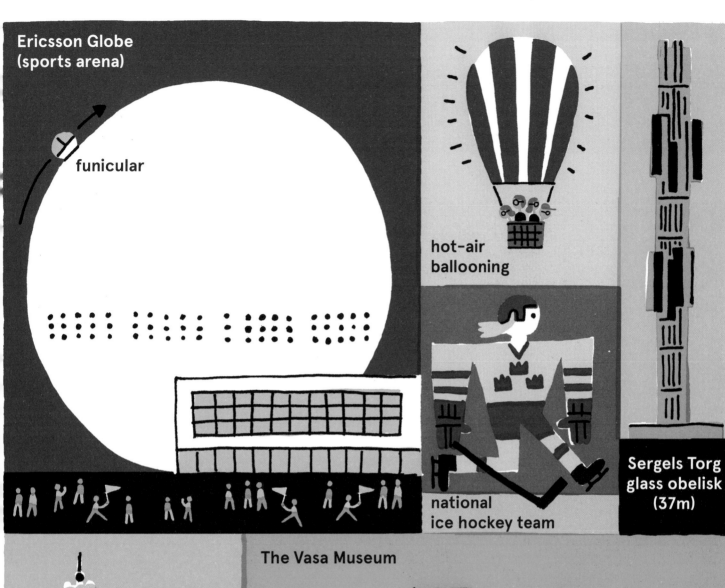

Ericsson Globe
(sports arena)

funicular

hot-air
ballooning

Sergels Torg
glass obelisk
(37m)

national
ice hockey team

colourful facades on
Stortorget Square

The Vasa Museum

17th-century Vasa Warship

MOSCOW

 14.8 million Russian ⚑ Russia

Bolshoi Theatre

St. Basil's Cathedral

ballet dancer

AND HOP!

Spasskaya Tower

Kremlin

Kremlin guard

Ostankino Tower (540m)

matryoshka (Russian dolls)

Gorky Park

blinis (stuffed pancakes)

Zhivopisny Bridge

hockey player

(television tower)

Metro

BARCELONA

 5 million   Catalan / Spanish   🏳 Spain

sculpture

Sagrada Família cathedral

football player

Joan Miró

tapas

lizard sculpture in Park Guell

Parc de la Ciutadella

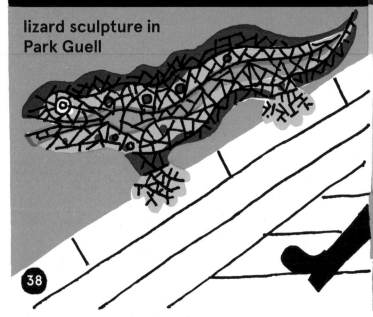

Torre Agbar skyscraper (144m)

FINALLY! I'VE REACHED THE TOP...

Montserrat mountain and monastery (45km north-west of city)

Picasso Museum

San Sebastián Beach

Mediterranean Sea

the Magic Fountain of Montjuïc

ROME

 4.3 million　 Italian　🏳 Italy

gelato (ice cream)

The Coliseum

according to legend, the Mouth of Truth bites the hand of liars

Italian scooter

The Panthéon

traffic policeman

Trevi Fountain

tomato and mozzarella pizza

LET'S GO!

small Italian car

Piazza del Popolo

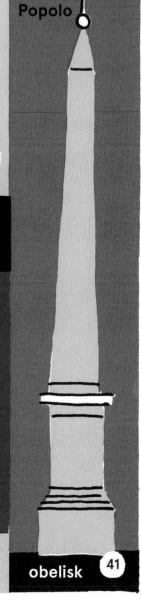

espresso coffee

Saint Peter's Basilica (Vatican)

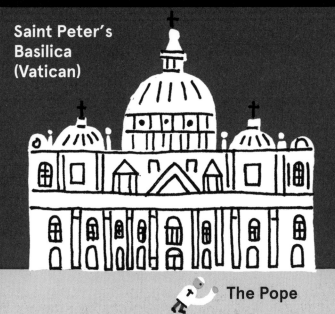

The Pope

obelisk

41

ATHENS

 3.8 million   💬 Greek   🏳 Greece

The Parthenon

KNOW THYSELF

Statue of Socrates

Acropolis of Athens

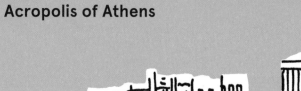

koulouri (sesame bagel)

historic area of Plaka

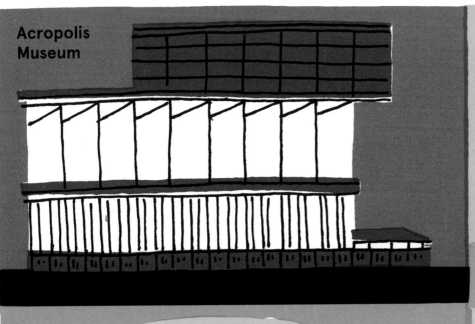

Acropolis Museum

Lycabettus Hill (277m)

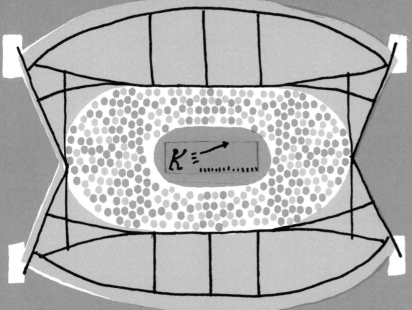

modern Olympic stadium (built in 1982)

travel by scooter

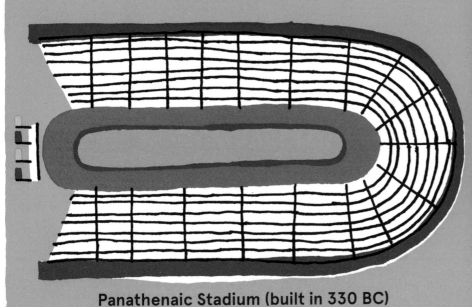

Panathenaic Stadium (built in 330 BC)

ANTIQUES! LOW PRICES!

Monastiraki Flea Market

43

ISTANBUL

👤 14.4 million   💬 Turkish   🚩 Turkey

Galata Tower (63m)

Blue Mosque

Museum of Modern Art

THIS PIECE OF ART IS MAKING ME HUNGRY!

loukoum

(Turkish delight)

Head of Medusa

Sunken Palace

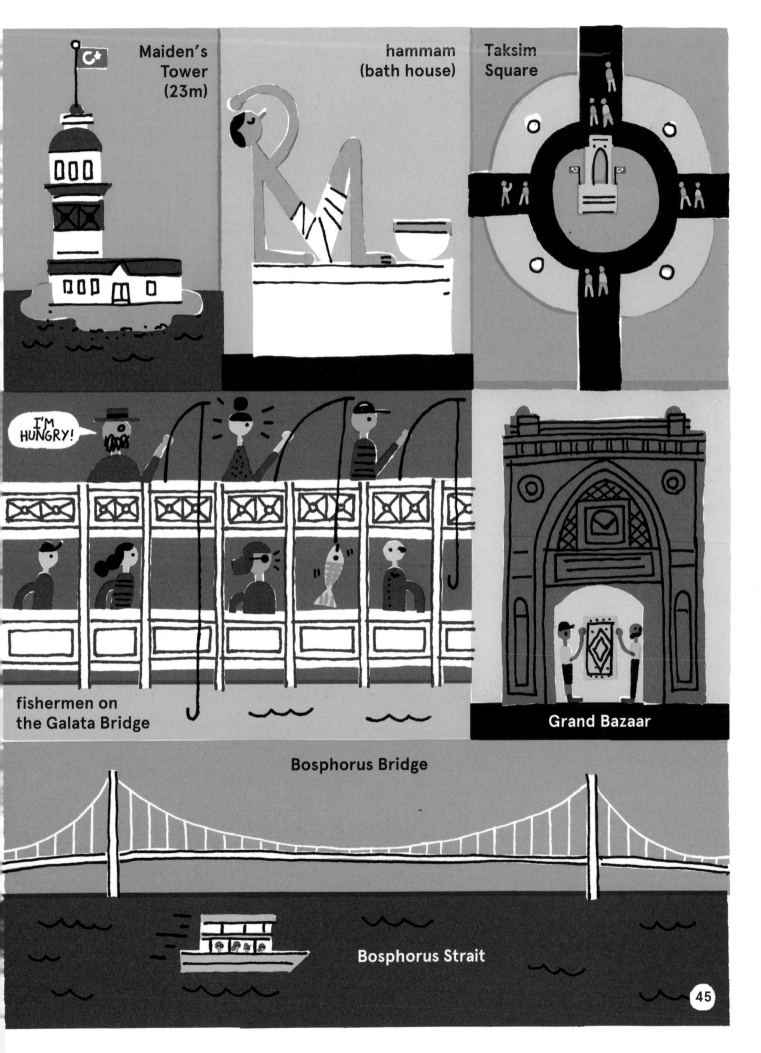

FEZ

👤 1.2 mil 💬 Arabic 🏴 Morocco

couscous dish

(served with meat and vegetables)

Bab Boujloud Gate

Minaret of Medersa Bou Inania

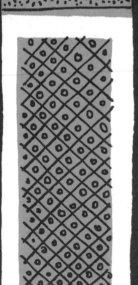

Royal Palace

Medina of Fez (ancient walled part of the city)

traditional
fountain

Fez tanneries

babouches
(typical
shoes)

at the souk (marketplace)

A PURE
DELIGHT!

mint tea

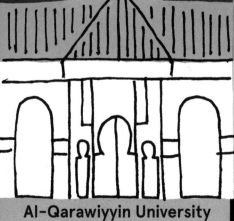

Al-Qarawiyyin University

PETIT TAXI

petit taxi
(small car
taxicab)

CAIRO

 20.4 million Arabic (Egyptian) 🏴 Egypt

Bab Zuwila Gate

Cairo Citadel

Al-Azhar Mosque

kochari (onions, pasta, lentils and rice)

Khan el-Khalili Souk

48

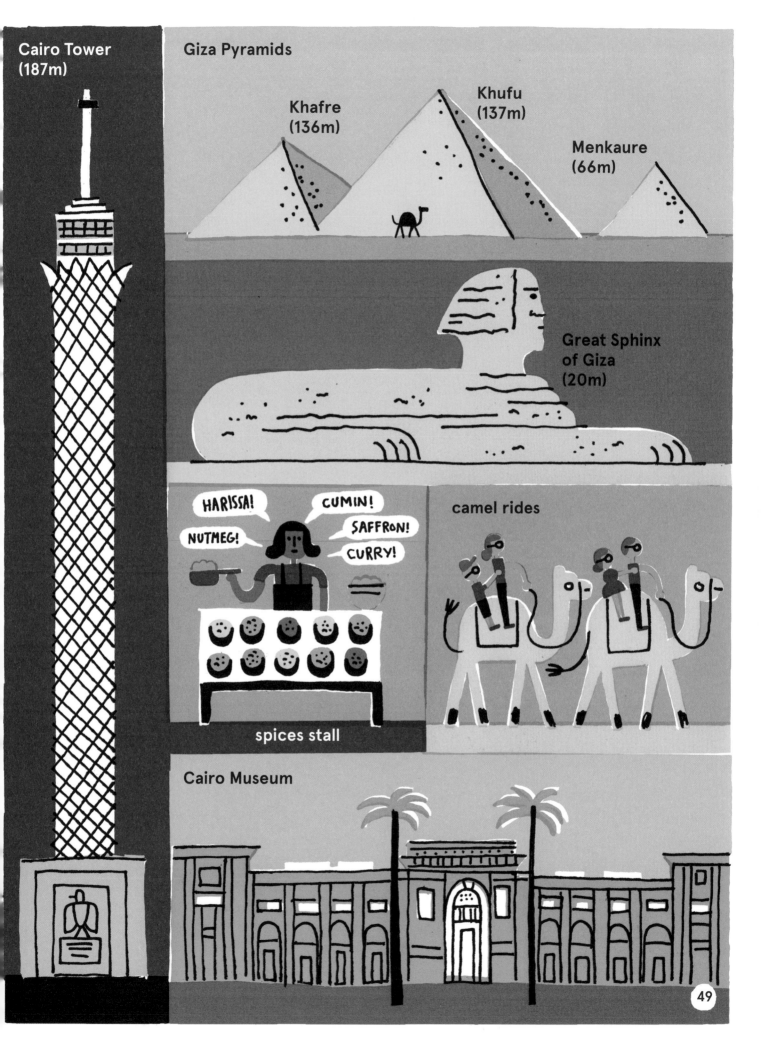

NAIROBI

 4.5 million　 English / Swahili　🏴 Kenya

Jamia Mosque

Uhuru Gardens

ride a matatu

sukuma wiki with chapati

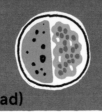

(cabbage, pancake and flatbread)

50

Kenyatta International Conference Centre (105m)

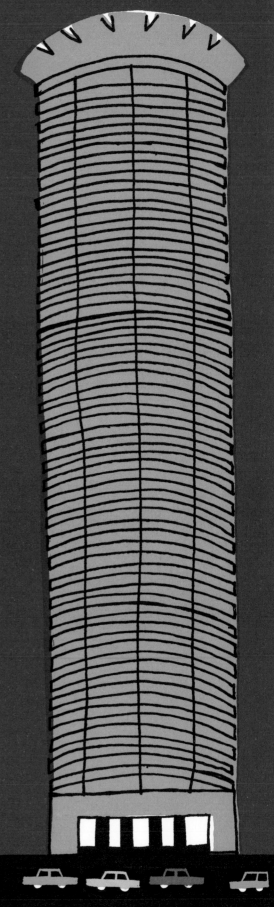

national park

Giraffe Centre

Ngong Hills wind farm

Nyayo Monument

dinosaur statue at the Nairobi National Museum

WOW!

Maasai Market

JOHANNESBURG

👤 8 million 💬 Nguni and Sotho languages / English / Afrikaans 🏴 South Africa

Orlando Towers in Soweto

statue of Nelson Mandela

A GREAT MAN!

rugby player

Nelson Mandela Bridge

biltong

(dried meat)

52

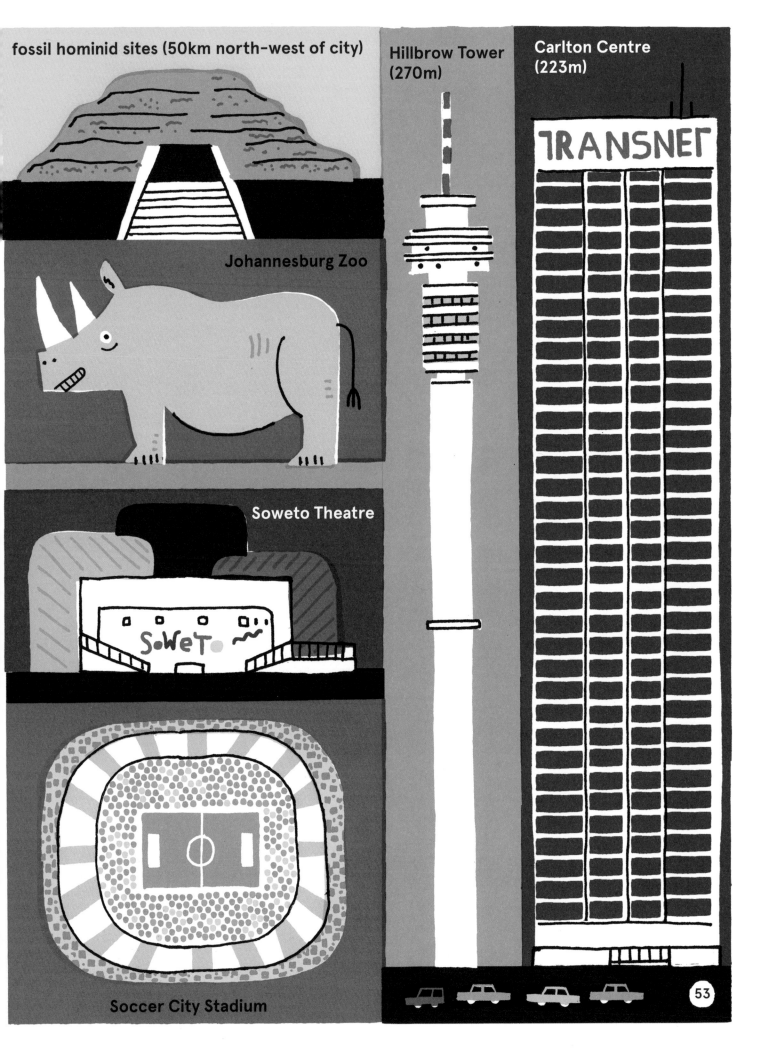

fossil hominid sites (50km north-west of city)

Johannesburg Zoo

Soweto Theatre

SOWETO

Soccer City Stadium

Hillbrow Tower (270m)

Carlton Centre (223m)

TRANSNET

MUMBAI

 21.9 million   Marathi   India

Ganesh statue (Hindu deity)

Siddhivinayak Temple

VROOOM

rickshaw

Haji Ali Dargah Mosque

Haji Ali Bay

Imperial Towers (254m)

Gateway of India

dahi puri (bread stuffed with potato)

Vipassana Pagoda

corn seller on the beach

Dharavi area

Elephanta Caves

BANGKOK

 18.9 million 💬 Thai 🏴 Thailand

Wat Arun (Temple of the Dawn)

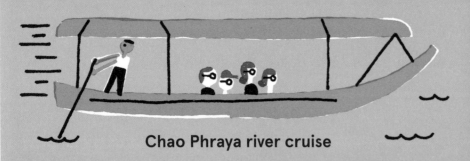

Chao Phraya river cruise

YUM!

fried beetles

tuk-tuk ride

Baiyoke Tower II (304m)

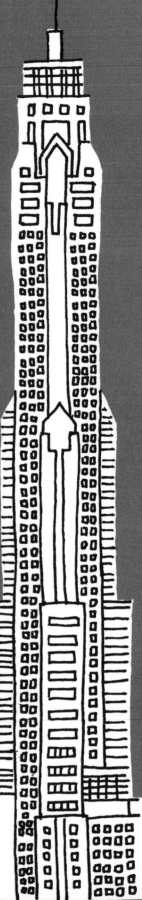

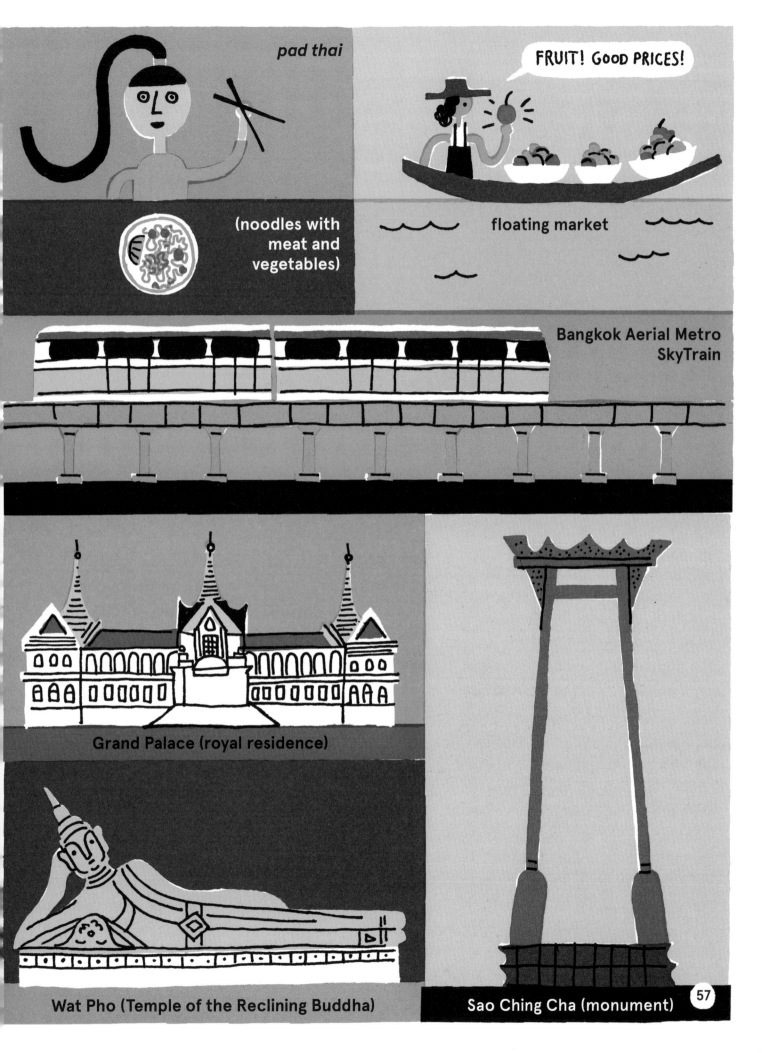

pad thai

(noodles with meat and vegetables)

FRUIT! GOOD PRICES!

floating market

Bangkok Aerial Metro SkyTrain

Grand Palace (royal residence)

Wat Pho (Temple of the Reclining Buddha)

Sao Ching Cha (monument)

HONG KONG

 9.6 million Cantonese / English ⚑ China

Sik Sik Yuen Wong Tai Sin Temple

Clock Tower (44m)

junk boat cruise

Star Ferry

jockey club

HERE I COME!

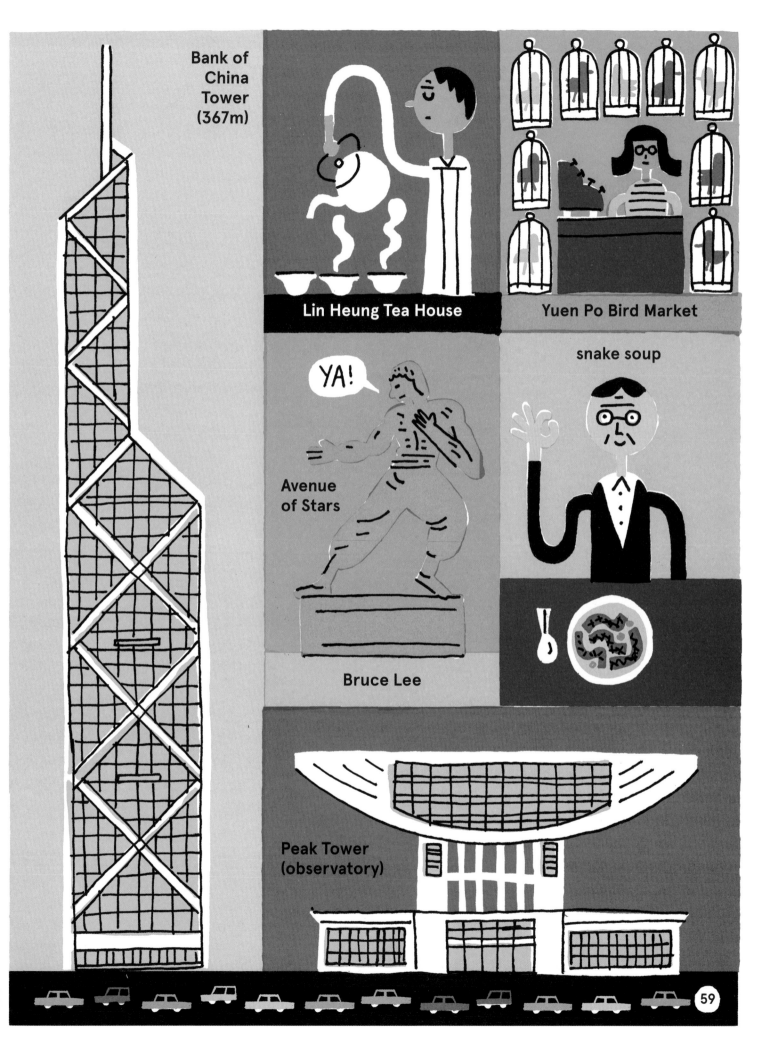

Bank of China Tower (367m)

Lin Heung Tea House

Yuen Po Bird Market

Avenue of Stars

Bruce Lee

snake soup

Peak Tower (observatory)

SEOUL

👤 25.6 million   💬 Korean   🚩 South Korea

Haechi statue

N Tower (237m)

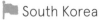

Gyeongbokgung Palace

Namdaemun Market

60

THIS PARK IS BEAUTIFUL!

bike ride in the Yeouido Park

Buddha statue at the Bongeunsa Temple

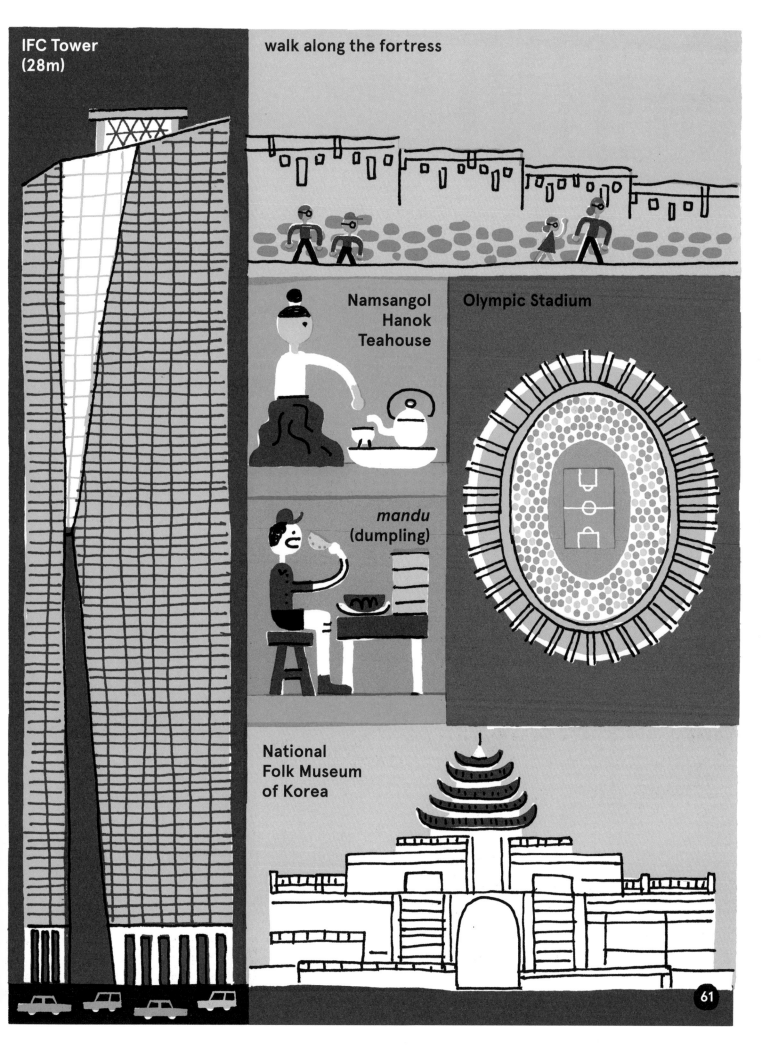

IFC Tower (28m)

walk along the fortress

Namsangol Hanok Teahouse

mandu (dumpling)

Olympic Stadium

National Folk Museum of Korea

TOKYO

 42.8 million   Japanese 🏳 Japan

baseball player

Tokyo Tower (333m)

Mount Fuji (3,776m)

ramen bowl

(noodle soup)

karaoke

Shinjuku Imperial Gardens

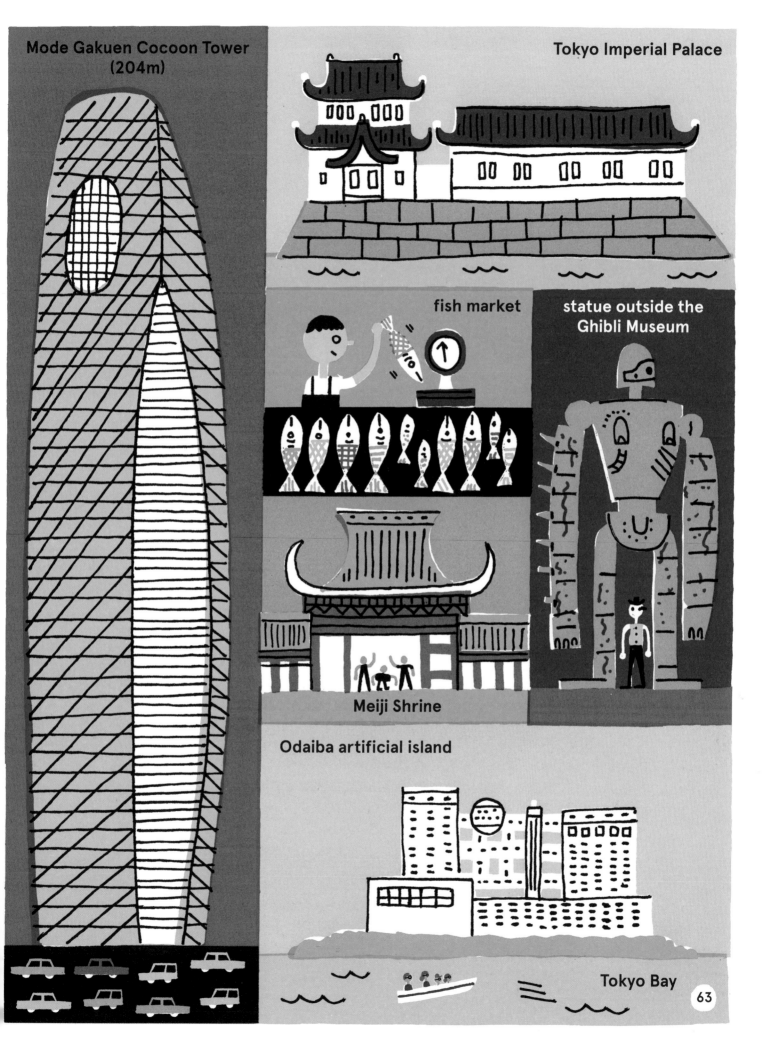

Mode Gakuen Cocoon Tower (204m)

Tokyo Imperial Palace

fish market

statue outside the Ghibli Museum

Meiji Shrine

Odaiba artificial island

Tokyo Bay

JAKARTA

 30.3 million 💬 Indonesian 🏳 Indonesia

Istiqlal Mosque

 gado gado

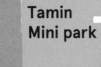 (salad with peanut sauce)

Tamin Mini park

National Monument (137m)

Dutch drawbridge (old town area)

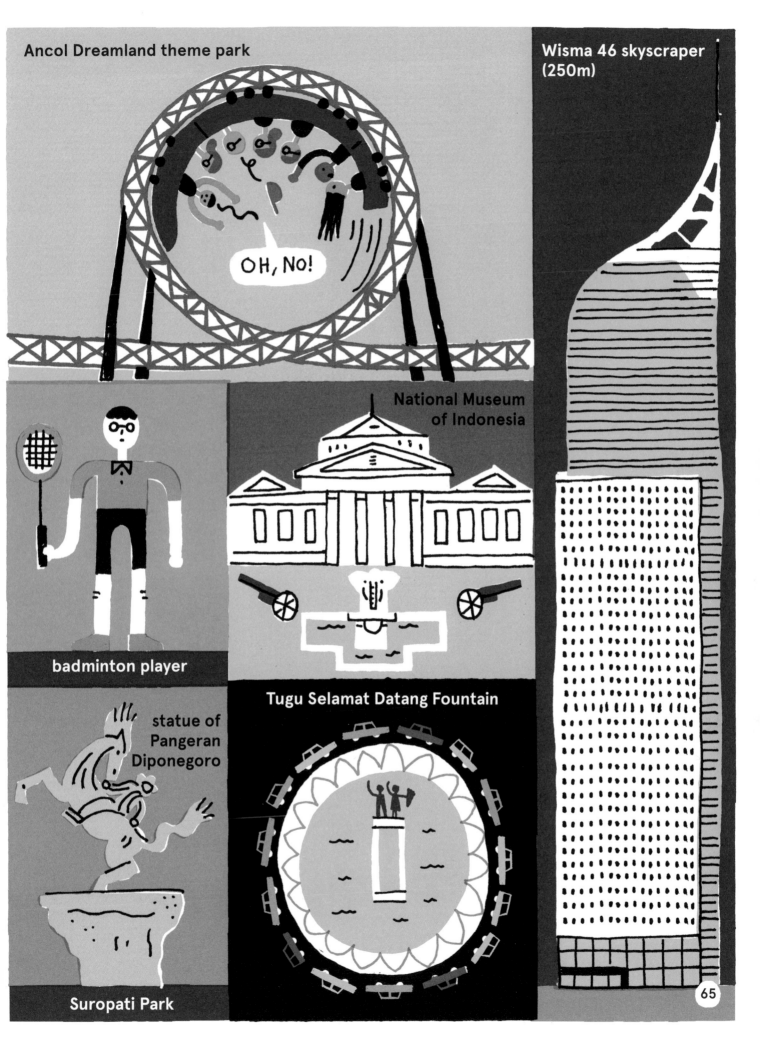

Ancol Dreamland theme park

OH, NO!

Wisma 46 skyscraper (250m)

badminton player

National Museum of Indonesia

statue of Pangeran Diponegoro

Tugu Selamat Datang Fountain

Suropati Park

SYDNEY

👤 4.7 million   💬 English   🏳 Australia

kookaburra

(Australia's national bird)

SYDNEY IS MY FAVOURITE CITY!

Sydney Harbour Bridge

Sydney Opera House

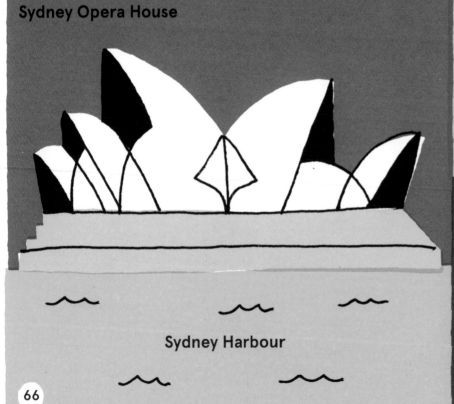

Sydney Harbour

harbour cruise

66

AUCKLAND

 1.4 million   English  New Zealand

**Sky Tower
(328m)**

**Auckland War
Memorial Museum**

pavlova
**(meringue,
whipped cream
and fruit)**

DELICIOUS!

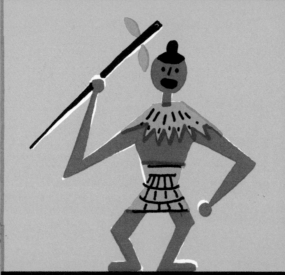

Tamaki Maori Village

Auckland Harbour Bridge

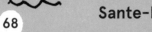

Sante-Marie Bay

68

ferry terminal

One Tree Hill and its obelisk

dolphin and whale tours

Piha beach

Rangitoto (volcanic island)

Hauraki Gulf

cricket player

69